Symphony in B Minor

Symphony

in B Minor

Pathétique

The Passion of Peter Ilitch Tchaikovsky

according to Larry Holdridge

A CONFESSION
FOR NARRATOR AND ORCHESTRA
IN FOUR MOVEMENTS

illustrations by Ferebe Streett

Owings Mills, Maryland
1978

Inquiries should be directed to
Stemmer House Publishers, Inc.
2627 Caves Road
Owings Mills, Maryland 21117

Photographs of pages from the score, in the composer's own hand, are reproduced from the facsimile in the Library of Congress, with permission. The original manuscript is in the collection of the Glinka Museum, Moscow.

A Barbara Holdridge book
Printed and bound in the United States of America
First Edition

Published simultaneously in Canada by George J. McLeod, Limited, Toronto

Library of Congress Cataloging in Publication Data

Holdridge, Lawrence B.
Symphony in B minor.
Poem.
1. Chaĭkovskiĭ, Petr Il'ich, 1840–1893, in fiction, drama, poetry, etc. I. Title.
ML64.H7 811'.5'4 78-2284
ISBN 0-916144-26-7
ISBN 0-916144-27-5 pbk.

This book is dedicated to
La Baigneuse Accroupie
Who showed me a Way through Never.

Symphony in B Minor

First Movement

So cosmic is thy loneliness, so god-like thy despair.

1.
Symphonie pathétique
I.
Adagio (♩ = 54)
Adagio (♩ = 54)
19097

Adagio

I had lived.

I had loved.

I had lost.

I was done.

Desolate

Disconsolate

Desperate

Alone

A portless ship on a sullen sea, with neverwhere a lengthening coast,
Nor might the craft's untended helm, a steady hand, her master's, boast.

Who will tell the footsteps vain,
Unnumbered milestones lately passed?
And who will chart the random wakes
That scar the ocean, endless, vast?

O do not mourn the loved dead,
The wandering winds in darkness lost,
But grieve for those the lost ones fled—
On silent seas forever tossed.

Black is the color of my true love's hair—
black are her coral lips and skin, once so fair—
black is the color of the snow on her grave—
black is the air in her sorrowing cave.
Entombed, immured, imprest beneath
the ponderous weight of glacial blue,
unrescued from the incubus
of hundred-centuried leaden sleep,
she lies within a deeper dream
from which the dreamer never wakes.

Can she who lived, so long be dead
The years implant a reasoned doubt
That light the living onetime shed
Can linger when the lamp is out?

O wild winter wind from the lean grave returning!
Soft summer sun in the long night burning!
Wave on the Time-Tide brutally breaking
On the high shore of memory, ruthlessly shaking
My clutch on life; the will to live
Engulfing, destroying. Nor may it give
The lasting solace of blackened ashes
But wet with death uncleanly washes
The vortexed soul in last surrender.
Do all the roads of all the world
Upon this empty plain converge,
Where twisted wraiths of burned-out nights
Enfleshed by phantom years emerge?
Hard-pressed against a final shore
And mantled by implacable darkness
That shakes the gates of Nevermore
And slags the plain in utter starkness.
A candle burns in tenebrae
And yet the Star is lost.
The waters whisper wordlessly,
The Star by stars is crossed.

Allegro ma non troppo

Who stays the hand of his cord would sever?
Who holds out hope—a way through never?
I walk a strange and broken land in dark and desolate Quintana Roo.
Aloof, alive, alone and grand, a towering Ash beside the flow—
A lonely Ash, the only Ash, eternal Mother of all the world.
Against the sky Her ancient limbs like mailed fists are hurled.
There is no light the dark to leaven,
Yet, lo, this Tree upholding heaven.
Her roots engird the planet's waist,
With strengthening hands its backbone braced.

A leaden sky sags overhead;
Withdrawn Her limbs, the sky was dead.
Beside Her feet the Nornir sit;
In cryptic verse their hands have writ
In runes on stone, forever unread,
Like alien shapes in the River's bed
To conn the course whereby we steer
Through heavens of hope, through fens of fear.
The whispering Water weaves a web of sound to soothe my errant ear;
The Tree is shackled to the Shore of Time's unending efflux clear,
Where yesterday and far tomorrow are lightly limned against the Stream.
Days will come and days will go, like gossamer cities in a dream.
Yet only on the threshold could a mortal's eye at all contain
What stirred the racial memory in the quiet corners of his brain.
The bifurcated limb that fell and burned a hole in primal sky—
To wood its flesh connected well, a million times removed, still I.
Can man forget the arboreal womb that formed with care his feeling flesh,
While holding seas, amorphous lands and frivolous air within its mesh?
Mother Tree! O Yggdrasill!
The heart and soul and mind of Earth,
Who split the seas and shaped the Shore
Ere man to God gave questioned birth.
When first this orb in fiery flux
Began to cool in lengthless space,
Thy mighty roots, great lines, appeared
Across the planet's half-formed face,
And from the depths of wayward seas
Thou raised the land that man would tread,
And yet, without an envelope,
As on the moon, the land was dead.
Thy questing branches the myriad particles
Of gay, itinerant atmospheres
Then plucked from space that an airless world
With sly, select, celestial snares
Might life entrap. The elusive force
Pervades all wandering sentient airs.
The winds that blew between the worlds
Thy sturdy branches roughly shook.
The wiltless withes that from them fell
In son-starved Earth a firm root took.

Each twisted twig, a dauntless urge,
An irrepressible force unseen,
To change and grow and multiply,
Inaugurate the reign of green.
And from the topmost lightest limb
The forked stick was let to fall,
Where on the ground it stood erect
And Man, as less, began withal.
The years are lost in aeons unreckoned,
As falling leaves to earth are beckoned.
A thousand lives incessant one,
Thy sons are many and still are one.
Te Rogamus Audi Nos!

Andante

I sing the song of a lonely heart,
Of empty nights, tormented days,
Of fruitless search in lands apart,
Of endless quest in olden ways.

A Star in the sky on a starless night,
Rayless sun of an erstwhile day
A face well seen though I lacked sight,
The unlit lamp of an antique way.

The runes of Urth are struck in stone. Verthandi's words are on her lips.
The graven past where Skuld unsaid, has set the stage where mankind trips.
O Mother-Tree, a woman's heart beats soft beneath Thy woody breast;
O Mother of me, I beg that heart to grant Thy son but one request.
I've known a land before this noon; I've felt the warmth of a younger sun;
I've loved a voice whose accents will beguile my ear till Death has won.
In the absence of angels the gods fashioned her
In their image and likeness though perfect they were.
And they bathed her in beauty mortal eyes scarce contained,
Which they made then their duty to preserve unprofaned.
And none but the brave and the best of the land
Who would honor her name might aspire to her hand.
La damoiselle élue like a cloudlet on high

Andte (♩ = 69)

incalzando

adagio

Corni

adagio

incalzando

Con sordini (teneramente, molto cantabile, con espansione)

(sordini)

Con sordini

Con sordini (teneramente, molto cantabile, con espansione)

Con sordini

Andte (♩ = 69)

Where the wind works its will
In the soft summer sky.
From the song of the lark they distilled the pure essence
To invest her sweet voice with its bright effervescence.
A tremble of strings, or the rustle of wings—
Forget what I will, I remember these things.

Long before our lips had met
Or shaped the words of love we spoke,
My heart was liquid in the warmth
With which her wondrous eyes caressed me.
The vibrant sweetness of her voice—
Dulcet as a lonely lute
That hangs the fabric of its song
Against the cheerless wilderness.
And once I watched the burnished bronze
Of setting Sun's reluctant rays
And knew he stole the rusty gold
While passing trusted through her hair.
O well do I remember, but so long a time ago,
I left her in a crystal cave and heard the West Wind moan
As soft her name it murmured, then in trauma left the shore
To wander o'er the darkened face of Earth forevermore—
On the edge of the world where restless seas
Whispered of warmth their childhood knew,
Where outstretched hands of stark, stripped trees
Reached in vain for vanished blue.
And like the wind that seaward fled
I too was set adrift,
But carried in a secret place the memory of her face.
I saw her portrait like a star
In every sunless sky
That roofed the countless times I crawled,
Unwalking, yet to die.
The River tastes forgotten shores,
And wells of centuries cleave between
The graven rocks and spoken word,
The pieces moved by hands unseen.
Thy tireless limbs the sky uphold. Thy mighty roots the Earth embrace.
Urtharbrunn's water wets Thy feet, reflects Thy lovely unseen face.

O give me strength to breast the Stream. Give me means to cross the Tide.
Permit a sail to pierce the veil where never before a craft has plied.

My Star in the sky on a starless night.
Rayless sun of an erstwhile day.
Pale silhouette evanescing from sight,
The unlit lamp of an antique way.

O Mother with hands in the deep tangled sky
And feet firmly fixed on the bordering shore,
From time's bitter flux let me taste the sweet drops
Of the once golden days of my lost Nevermore.

Moderato mosso

Though warm the night, an icy Wind was stirred to restless, sudden life,
A Wind that tramped the outer void, whose breath cut like a surgeon's knife.
The Ash's limbs the bright Wind touched with questing fingers from Arcturus
And wafted down from pinnate leaves their soft and scarcely heard susurrus—
At first inarticulate, quickly particulate, sound of the whispering Tree.
The whisper grew stronger, the accents were longer—Yggdrasill was speaking to me.

In a drowsy world of steaming mists a million years ago
I set in earth the forked stick, a seed called Man, to grow.
The wind-burned branch, the wide-band bark, the strands of sylvan hair,
My sons arose from red-dawn dust to validate their hard-won share.
I loved them all, but none so well as Man, my favored child,
And him I raised to primacy, ascendant o'er the wild.
Urtharbrunn poured its ages slow; the conqueror of the main
Turned never once in all the flow to seek the Dweller on the plain.
He knelt at altars white and gold, his Maker while denied;
The Tree of Life he has disowned, destroy it even tried.
His astigmatic vision saw the untrod snow upon the peaks;
His necromantic fission now the magic mountain's stomach seeks.
He wends his ways in three directions, not suspecting, caring less,
That all his roads have this dimension, and lacking it were nothingness.
To stay the hand I could not fend at length the Nornir fair I bore,
Who, thrice select, might well protect the woody Plant astride the Shore.
I lost them to the River's glass; therein they found their rightful home;
With words of light reformed the night; ordained the shape of things to come.

O prisoners three, chained to a Tree, yet by the shifting River claimed!
Their Word was Will, to represent the world in watery canvas framed.
I've known the brooding heartache of a million years alone—
The only face to look upon, reflection of my own.
The painful barb lodged deep within my ancient wooden heart:
That Man was my delinquent child—how like a poisoned dart.
Now comes at last a member of the Tree-forgetting race,
Who addresses me as Mother, though never seen my face.
For dolorous years I've waited long for Man to recognize
The fount of his creation, strong, all-loving, just and wise.
I've looked into thy heart, my son. I'm awed by what is there—
So cosmic is thy loneliness, so godlike thy despair.
A part of me, yet part of thee, will take thee ages back—
A craft to ply the River Time, nor motive power will lack.
And wherewith that to swift propel, this slender branch accept
To send thee fast and send thee well, ten thousand years o'erleapt.
May thy quest know happy ending. May thy love at last thee find.
Let thy astral journey wending soon bring peace thy troubled mind.

The susurration faded, then was lost in still night air.
The wandering wind forsook the Tree. The answer to my prayer—
Her flesh and blood, eternal wood, was lying on the shore.
I knelt on earth and kissed Her roots. Could I have asked for more?
The limb was hollow, tapered, long, a kind of crude canoe,
The chariest chip that ever sailed with mortal for a crew.
The silence hard upon me bore. I looked with fear into the Sea
That spun dark aeons by the score and wove them into eternity.
And Time was Then and Time was When and Time will even ever be
The temporal template clamped across the craft that sail the sightless Sea.
The vortex spawned its tiny ships in widening circles turning slow,
The swirling Flood a potter's wheel that shaped them with its cunning flow.
Upstream intrepid hulls set sail, their valiant sheets against the sky.
The White Wind laughed. I heard the gale remark how well men learned to die
From tetherless reaches of weatherless beaches that wing the world of long ago.
Across the plain, a Tree's domain, the River pours its endless flow
In Time-Not-Yet, wherein beget the nights and days and yearning years,
The sevenside sorrows of too many tomorrows, the whitewind woes and telltale tears.
Now wet with Time, my timeless craft was pitched against the strangest Stream—
From Mother Tree, an ancient graft to incarnate the impossible dream.
Below the Limb of Yggdrasill uncounted lifespans fanned astern
The whispered promise to fulfill, a hundred centuries swift return.

O Mother with hands in the deep tangled sky
And feet firmly fixed on the bordering shore –
From time's bitter flux let me taste the sweet drops
Of the once golden days of my lost nevermore.

Adagio mosso

Atop the world, with time to bide, the King of Kryochore
The beckoning Warmlands southward eyed and planned that lightning war
Should paralyze his lifelong foe, the burning brilliant Sun,
And extirpate the Shining One, his reign of warmth be done.
To doctrines of eternal ice and everlasting snow
The Southlands turned unhearing ears and let the Ice-Winds blow.
For here lived beings whose blood was warm, tall trees and scented flowers,
The lord of these was safe from harm and basked in sunlit hours.
The Sun supplied all things and more, and cared for what he planted,
But while the Cold fomented war, he took the Sun for granted.
When came the Night, Sun left perforce his undisputed throne;
His pallid Queen for him would rule the kingdom vast alone.
When Morning had the Night dispersed, his Queen would shy retire,
A sceptre fearless Sun would wield, the world light with his fire.
For centuries long his radiance unchallenged far or near,
Sun failed to note the King of Ice no longer stood in fear.
His strength the Torngat had amassed through years of patient toil,
His icy armies seething now the Warmlands to despoil.
Then quickly frigid tentacles a Southland overran,
But tiny and defenseless, not important in Sun's plan.
Elated by the ease with which his conquest had succeeded,
The Cold One made another grab—Sun's boundaries receded.
For time not long the inexorable march the Arctic Circle halted;
A few years passed. Across the line the Ice King one day vaulted.
And Sun was wroth that anyone should challenge his command.
The Torngat calmed him, promising, "This is my last territorial demand."
And one by one the Warmlands of the South were overrun
By icy hosts. The King of Ice at length had stopped the Sun.
"From warm sanguinity we carve our realm, laid to last ten thousand years;
A Lebensraum for supermen, the Nordic gods their only peers."
Belatedly the Sun prepared for vastly escalated war,
But on his face appeared a spot, at first a small and running sore.
The brightness of his warbeams thus by sickly sunspots rendered futile,
The southward march of Snow and Ice was unrelenting, blind and brutal.

Allegro vivo

The wave that endlessly rolls out of an infinite far horizon
And spends itself on little feet against a present shore
Had beached the craft that scorned the stars and left me midst the strife
That laid an iron hand across the schizoid land that gave me birth.

The universe is many things to God and man and blade of grass.
Unpictured canvas, formless stone, unsounded notes and words unspoke,
O'ershadowed, stark and unfulfilled, to each it holds a beckoning glass,
Where man, like God, exerts his will, that strangest mix of dark desire,
By all the frantic fires of love and hate and hope and fear incended,
To clothe with flesh, pervade with blood, enform and craft the willowing bone,
On woven cloth, vibrating air, on white unyielding amorphous stone.
Dream, as such, does not exist. Creation, bloody-pawed,
Now stands erect and celebrates the marriage of the bear.
God may dream and split the sun,
And from the fragments build His garden,
But man can split the eye of God
And shape the shards into a woman.

Is beauty's outline molded by profane or sacred hands?
Or is her portrait painted in the beholder's loving eye?
The sound of music shakes the air that leaves unshook a lonesome drum.
The fathering ether springs the song no sentient ear would dare contain.
Without an end, without beginning, a careless *son et lumière*
Has filled the eyeless heart of night with warp and weft to weave the welkin.
The pale fire, the fledgling fancy, the joyous lilt in laughing air,
The amaranthine alluvion in the swirling seething Sea of Time.

A rusty gold enframed the face that launched in pain the Time-borne ship.
Could all the wealth of Earth replace the merest smile upon her lips?
Not all the pearls beneath the seas
Nor golden veins that seam our mountains;
Not all the spices of the East
Nor perfumed waters of her fountains.
Our separate eyes behold two scenes
That summed as one enrich our seeing.
Each alien heart requires another
To live and move and have its being.

And kings were made and kings were born to sit the Warmland's crumbling throne;
A fallen despot's mantle shorn I seized, proclaimed his seat my own,
Then sought to hold my newly won against the menace to the north;
Too late. The Torngat's armies had already sallied southward forth.
We might have stopped the King of Ice had wall-like union been displayed,
But turncoat Winter to the foe our deepest differences betrayed.
Four columns cold from Ice Land struck; the Fifth, within, disclosed itself;
Chameleonic Winter to our detriment disposed himself.
The rain that once with gentle drops had nursed the fertile suckling soil
With steely barbs of ice destroyed the greening products of her toil.
The gentle breeze that lightly breathed across the Warmland's upturned face,
Now blasted wide the startled skies and emptied heaven of sunlight's trace.
The blow was hard, the timing sure; the war was ruthless, lightning-swift.
Defenseless, dazed, we found ourselves a broken people set adrift.
Our fragile homes, for sun designed, no match for Ice Land's withering blast.
Our raiment light, yet unresigned, we fought the Ice King to the last.

How quickly drained the precious cup that tens of centuries took to fill!

The decimated remnant of the God- and sun-forsaken lost,
Led by a king in whom all eyes invested now their failing vision,
Not to stay the blue-boned hand, but seek the road of royal rout
O'er which a wounded, beaten Sun had painfully dragged his shattered rays.
Air and Water, Earth and Fire—of these the world constructed,
But now replaced by isotopes from God's white hell eructed:
Chill, whose torpid touch congealed the flesh-and-blood-protected marrow;
Cold that seared like burning flame the tempered tools of locomotion;
Snow, the obverse face of rain, its vampire lust by white concealed;
Ice, the crystal harlot from whose shelled embrace no man escapes.

The gray constrictor sheet had crushed the living green from leaves of grass.
Its frigid fingers slew the air and squeezed its corpse to powdered glass
That scratched the eyes and set the face and filled the lungs with molten fire.
Judicare saeculum per ignum. The words were uttered by a Liar.

The old ones froze as their blood ran slow;
We left them, statues, in the silence of the snow.
Talwyn kissed her child's curled head;
The wind kissed both. The two were dead.
A pattern of red on the glistering white,

Orchid-eyed skulls in the black of night,
Vanquished green and vanishing blue,
Burned-out gold in the dawn's gray hue.

Our starving herds we kept alive to conservate their animal heat.
The want of warmth was more acute than even the need of nourishing meat.
Yet chill that charged their caprine bone
Turned pulsing hearts to arctic stone.
Their flesh we flensed like birds of prey
To vain postpone the approaching day
When Cold with Hunger shared his loot—
From the Tree of Life the rigid fruit.
The cryogenic hours of day had sired the silence that was night.
Death found his mark with greater ease when we were robbed of sound and sight.
Each morning as the Sun would rise, a wan and distant glow,
We told our dead in dark despair and buried them in the snow.
No where to turn, to no one pray—the stricken sought Ethweyn.
Her merest touch, her slightest smile, anesthetized their pain.
In the absence of angels they settled for her,
Content in her presence, condemned as they were.

The lunar wheel had turned again. With cold objective gaze
The Moon looked down without a trace of heavenly compassion,
And watched the white, distracted night play out the final phase
Where Yggdrasill's embattled sons had loved Her in their fashion.
Pockmarked and disfigured by the meteoric waste
Flung without concern by careless Hands from outer space,
Airless and cold,
Frustrated and old,
A smile of satisfaction wreathed her proud but bitter face.

The Apocalyptic Horsemen sallied forth from Hell below.
The white and red, the black and pale threw shadows on the snow.
There was no hurry. They could wait. They knew our herds were gone.
My ranging spear a mastodon then felled to earth at dawn.
The creature vast by starlight dim his hunter did not see;
No telltale wind befriended him to warn of lurking me.
The hand that held salvation's spear knew well it dared not miss.
It clove the air with flint-tipped death; the mammoth breathed a hiss.
He died with one convulsive throe; perhaps he too was tired

Of cloying ice and clinging snow, no more to live aspired.
The fallen giant's still-warm flesh contained the merest hint
We might perchance elude the cold, escape by sheerest dint.
But rage is like the salts of lead and stores inside the poisoned heart
Till press within compels it shed its bonds and tear the earth apart.
When Night her cloak of frozen stars for the scanty scarf of Morning traded,
The hope of reaching warmth afar in dawn's white waxing quickly faded.
The icen-armored vanguards pressed our backs against the sullen sea.
Swift glacial blue then intercepted all attempts to southward flee.
But as we queued along the beach, fast fishing craft like chips emerged
To whisk some far beyond the reach of bergs from shoulders down submerged.
I sought a secret solace in this frantic flight from force titanic—
The ebbing tide one day returned by greater forces oceanic?
The cliffs of chalk were moving now, impelled by frozen, mobile rivers.
The Earth itself was on the march, in metered tread, iambic quivers.
Stalactites sharp, like teeth of glass, the wind-wiped seashore harshly harrowed.
The flowing Cold's advancing mass our fading foothold numbly narrowed.
We stared into the moving wall that trapped our gaze in shards opaque,
And held it, though reluctant, as a charmer holds a charmed snake.
A tremor traced the stricken strand; the Earth was rent asunder.
The fall of ice was quickened and the heavens split with thunder.
Gorged with ice and sick unto death,
The torn terrene convulsed for breath,
Writhed in pain and clenched its fists,
Scythed like grain by glacial twists,
Coughing and spitting and vomiting white,
Sloughing and splitting its blanket of blight
Till impotent Sun's empathic eye
Saw most of the last in rigor die.

Where the Warm Wind walked the White Wind struck
And left her lifeless in the crackling air.
The Southland's rose had fled her cheek,
The Cold had claimed my faltering fair.
They say the dream can never die unless the cup is underfilled.
I call on heaven to hear my cry: my Lord and God has overkilled.

Andante come prime

O Star in the sky on a starless night!
Rayless sun of an erstwhile day.
Pale silhouette so white on white,
Extinguished lamp of an antique way.

The runes of Urth are struck in stone;
Verthandi's words are on her lips;
The graven past where Skuld unsaid
Has set the stage where mankind trips.
What end this strength that streaked the Stream?
What worth this craft that crossed the Tide?
What God-begotten monstrous scheme
Attests the fact that God has lied?
"Dum veneris judicare,
Judicare saeculum per ignum."
But in my arms embodied dreams
Are cold
And still
And dead.
No Sun in the heavens.
No Star in the sky.
The light of my living
By God bereft I.

My Star in the sky on a starless night.
Rayless Sun of an erstwhile day.
Pale silhouette on the evering white
The unlit lamp of an antique way.

Telluria's lights are flickering out
In all but the warmest clime.
Nor are they destined to be relit,
To shine again within our time.
In the granite of water enslaved by Cold I carved a niche and crudely fashioned
A place to rest my love of loves and leave my heart with grief impassioned.
On the edge of the world where restless seas whispered of warmth their childhood knew,
Where outstretched hands of stark, stripped trees reached in vain for vanished blue,

I laid my love in a crystal cave and kissed her fair and marble brow.
The West Wind moaned o'er the salt sea wave and eavesdropped on my farewell vow.

O love, for me you were a door,
A path, a stair, an opened room,
A cooling draft for burning thirst,
A blaze of light that follows gloom.
Can I have ever possessed you and yet by you be unpossessed?
Can Earth retain the silvery moon and yet her love be unconfessed?
The flowers I have planted can never die or wither away.
The songs I sang for you alone I'll sing again another day.
The blossoms broken by the Cold will bloom some random raptured Spring.
My scattered songs will once return like homing birds on welcome wing.
But I must die a hundred times to know that death can never last—
The future's soaring castles built with stones and mortar from the past.
And so the rose by other names is still a rose and smells as sweet,
The dreaded noumenon we fear but footfalls on a two-way street.

O sleep now, my beloved,
Let peace and rest your consorts be.
And never a dream disturb your sleep—
Not even the smallest dream of me.
Be still and wait, who knows how long?
Benumbed, perhaps, ten thousand years
Till fair Telluria smiles again
And Sun has thawed her frozen tears.
If well your name is treasured in the lonely temple of my heart,
Its sound will lie on all the lips that speak for unborn hearts to come.
A Wind is rising, small of voice, but fathered by the farthest Sun;
It blows its breath beneath the ground. I give the wandering Wind my tongue
To spread in every corner of a whitened, disenlightened Earth
The legend of your dark eclipse, the promise of your bright rebirth.
The River spends its years yet keeps the substance spent in timeless deeps.
No counted hour is ever lost.
The prow that broke the astral plain returns one day this world to gain,
Uncounted power is never crossed.
The blooms of Spring are tightly curled to bear the weight of Winter's snow.
This arilled grot, this remnant world, will turn the edge of Ice Land's blow.
In this tight niche to slumber then, nor stir nor wake until the day
When Ice has melted, Snow has vanished, conquering Cold is put away.

When rising Sun, a world reborn, will joyous herald the splendid morn,
The brave new Kingdom, Power and Glory, the Promised Land foretold in story.
A rock in Time, by Time untouched, of hopes and dreams the total sum,
You are the light alluvion to rise enisled one day to come.
Dies irae dies illa, solvet saeculum in favilla.
Rest, my love, in peace and sleep,
Dreamless,
Gleamless,
Themeless
Sleep.
Sleep my Star—
Sleep my Sun—
Sleep—
S
L
E
E
P

Second Movement

The tramping stars at perihelion seek to check
their coursing flight,
To bask awhile upon the hearth and burn the
cold from astral bone;
A pause before departure into silent and
unpeopled Night,
On wheeling orbits, frozen-waked, they take
their shivering way alone.

II

Allegro con grazia (♩ = 144)

Fl. I
Fl. II
Fl. III (Picc.)
Oboi
Cl. I in A
Cl. II
Fagotti
Corni F.
Trombe A
3 Tromboni e Tuba
Timp. A, D, E
V. I
V. II
Vle
Cel.
Cb.

Allegro con grazia

Allegro con grazia

The seconds make the minutes make the hours make the days;
The cycle of the moon will mark the circle of the sun;
The golden circle's tightly woven scintillating rays
In patterns of a hundred wake the meteoric run
Of timeless wood, the flesh and blood of an ancient, ageless Tree
Who lent Herself that a woeful son of a race now self-enslaved,
Though mortal born, might fearless scorn the endless, evering Sea,
And find his own salvation in a course not yet engraved.
The paddle slips through unnamed years and lightly drips with days and nights;
The wind that wore all yesterdays now breathes upon the turgid Tide
And lifts in droplets self-contained, the essence each of all delights,
Expanded Am, perspectived Was, a dreaming realm of Now inside.
The wind is old, and the wind is cold and delves dark depths of the somnolent Sea;
In watery laminations flips like cards each scarred and scarlet sheet
Where History's hand in fast-dried ink of swiftly flowing fleeting hours
Has writ the page that ever returns, its unlearned lessons to repeat.
Across the umbered lang lay leaves the Horsemen Four had left their mark—
An oft-repeated motif, like a scourge upon our hapless race
That felt the icy template twice before the whirling world went dark,
Yet lived to forge still-heavier chains its frigid fetters to replace.
The fairest parts of Earth may writhe beneath the tyrant's heedless heel;
Extinguished by his chilling breath, the light of learning disappear;

And megalomania's hand, a brake, restrain the forward-turning wheel.
The darkened lands are yet reborn; the promised Sun will reappear.
How serves the serf save through his faith he one day doubtless will be free—
To fill his lungs with freedom's air, to speak forbidden thoughts aloud,
For God nor man no cap in hand, for kings and thrones no bended knee,
Decatenate his feudal state and walk erect with head unbowed.
And yet the serf too long may serve, his wavering will to freedom break,
Like caged birds whose grates ajar in uncaged sunshine feebly flutter
And spread their pindle-feathered wings in vain the tenuous air to take,
Then tiring seek their stinking cage. The weight of serfdom's chains is better.
And sons of slaves get sons of slaves. Beneath the bowl of heaven's blue
The floor of hell is raised by man to make his footing all more certain.
Expedience is deified; he cannot tell the false from true;
For Truth is dead and Honor fled behind the manmade metal curtain.
And outside, fearful Freedom sits, with nervous fingers hefts a sword
Of steel not forged, but strangely bright, the stuff of distant light-wrought stars,
Unruly protons held in check, awaiting but the whispered word
To strip of strength the curtain's length and geld the god of wanton wars.
Strike first, O Freedom! Sword in hand, strike first lest thee be basely stricken,
As once a lustrous inlet felt the force of oriental fury.
The time has come for gods to act, their pulses all serene must quicken;
The Stream is slow, but History's flow is redly written in a hurry.
Where people say, their voices raise a shining spire against the sky.
Beware the angry little men who honeycomb its splendid walls,
Like termites boring from within, and tunneling earthward lest they die,
They'll raise a darkened dungeon where the hard-won house of free men falls.
The mall that looses streams of sweat would likewise loose a crimson flood
When wedded to the sickle's steel that fells the grain for daily bread.
What monstrous children march beneath the banner of the Cult of Blood,
Who seek to raise their order on dissenting bones of brethren dead?
Must all of Earth be cloven into slavers and enslaved?
Marks every stone the Nornir cast a changeless course engraved?
Each rising sun must also set? The fens of darkness must be braved?
The best of men, the last of men, can none of them be saved?
The Tree is not the maker of the two-edged multicolored fates
That tinge the restless Tide that shapes the man-wakes on the uncouth Sea.
The sorry Seer only, having bore her sons free-willed, awaits
The passage of their tiny ships as each puts out intrepidly.

He may not choose the deck he walks, nor yet select the wind-filled sheets
That bend the masts that leave all Pasts and sail him swiftly into Here;
He can't predict the wind's caprice, the whims of weather that he meets;
His craft is frail, but this is sure: that man alone his ship will steer.
The acts that leave their print on Time are surcharged by the acts not done,
The stratification of Now on Then to lay a couch for wispy When,
Of metered seconds, fractioned hours and arcs of circles 'round the sun,
Where man expired before his birth, inspired, perspired and lived again.
Now see the painful pageant of a thousand lives incessant one,
Their sprawling structures raised upon foundations often ill-begun.
The Old is Change; the Change is New; there's nothing old beneath the sun;
The whirling world its wonders works, as if by will. Whose Will be done?
And Whose the Kingdom and the Power, and Whose the many-sided Glory?
Detached, aloof, affected not by slicing Time, encroaching Space,
Who, having writ the opening page, must write the last one in the story,
At every turn reveals His hand, without concern conceals His face.
O do not seek the gentle rains or sultry sunshine freely given.
The seed within the stranger's breast by heavenly manna is not nourished,
And cannot thrive if sharply from connecting bone its roots are riven;
The blackened blooms on every vine attest the hopes that might have flourished.
Six thousand golden circles mark man's search in vain of empty skies
For answer to the unanswered he might find behind unseeing eyes.
He seeks his handmade image when the winged life within him flies
But does not die in permanence; his white reflection only dies.
The double helix sparks the round. His life and death and certain birth
A process of refining that includes the whole of teeming Earth;
Its ferreting fingers grasp the smallest blade of greenly growing grass,
The lucent drops of water in Telluria's lonely oceans vast.
A subtle sequence of mutation unperceived at living range,
As insects on a painting can but lumps of bright-hued pigment see,
Participating, contemplating not the magnitude of change,
He lacks the Time-perspective that alone would set enslaved man free.
Yet, in his sorties on the Sea, a man by random finger chosen,
Projects in interrupted frames a record of bathymetry.
Both sum and product of his years, the pristine, crystalline distillation
Now gently holds the Time-wise eye with finely wrought magnificence.
Within the Water's luminous depths a shining mirror brightly held
To show each line and shadow-year in History's wan and careworn face.
Both peasants' lives and kings' archives in panorama tightly jelled,
The long-since dead are now alive; unpausing Time flows on apace.

The road is marked by stony runes that trap intact a minor eddy,
A backwash where in somnolence the Time-forgot might centuries lie,
Then yield like iron to lodestone's wiles, succumb at length to sightless steady
Attraction peristaltic of the Stream where none may lastly die.
Caesurae mark each separate line. A well of years may intervene
Where once he breathed and whence he breathed. As leaves that leave the topmost limb
Are long sustained in planless air, then spiral earthward, vanished green
And falling lone, touch lower leaves that join them in the interim.
The tramping stars at perihelion seek to check their coursing flight,
To bask awhile upon the hearth and burn the cold from astral bone,
A pause before departure into silent and unpeopled night,
On wheeling orbits, frozen-waked, they take their shivering way alone.

O magic Limb, unfettered by demand of days or press of hours,
Respond as light through darkness leaps, a thing alive beneath my hand,
And swift elude tempestuous Now where clouded Past-Time beetling lowers,
To straightway seek the lifted isle that looks upon the ice-bound strand
Where lies in deepest slumber, she whom Death had sought in final claim,
Yet found his grasping fingers stayed by force with which he could not cope,
A faith that rode the centuries and kept alive a woman's name,
A faith that fought with weapons gone, when all was lost excepting hope.

Now speed thee, craft, the Waters part, the winged paddle lightly drips;
Across the tens of hundred arcs the timeless bark now whitely skips.

Third Movement

Can swift Aurora's magic wood against the ice prevail?
Can Yggdrasill's enchanted Limb the Frozen Fort assail?

III

Allegro molto vivace (♩. = 152)

Fl. I
Fl. II
Piccolo
Oboi
Cl. I in A
Cl. II
Fag.

Corni in F
Trombe A
3 Tromboni e Tuba
Timp.

Allegro molto vivace (♩. = 152)

Violini I divisi
Viol. II divisi
Viole divise
Celli divisi
Bassi divisi

All^ro molto vivace (♩. = 152)

Allegro molto vivace

The *Aurora* lay at anchor in the port of Seven Star.
The quay was thronged with curious who knew she voyaged far

To lands away in Snow and Ice, to lands beyond the blue
Horizon where Unknown began, to where there sailed but few.

A ripple of excitement spread across the tiny bay;
The great *Aurora*'s sailing was the topic of the day.

In little knots the children and in larger groups the men
Conferred about the voyage and the why and where and when.

I think she sails tomorrow—I think she sails at dawn.
The eastern sky will lighten when the wind is fresh and strong.

Her skipper must be crazy, and a crazy crowd her crew.
The rats have left *Aurora* if the things they say are true.

Her master sails to find a girl a-frozen in the ice;
They say the frozen princess once was, yes, the master's wife!

Now how in all creation could a princess ever be
Ten thousand years a-frozen, yet alive like you or me?

A strange one there, the master, seems he hardly says a word,
Yet never from his purpose has he ever been deterred.

And up and down the fishing pier, across the land-locked bay,
A rumor jostled legend, and the rumor gave away.

For legend seemed to have it (it was written in a Stream)
That from the port a sailing man would sail to find his queen.

A single Star where stars are none, a burning flame where yet no sun;
The Truth perceived, though sight were lacked; of fadeless dreams the embodied act.

The Seeker draws the Seeking as the Sun will take by hand
His charge of wandering planets and together as a band,

Though separately involved, will sift the ash of outer space
Beneath the North Star's frozen smile to find their rightful place.

And to him came unanchored men, the flotsam of the seas,
The tumbleweeds of empty plains, the stands of rootless trees.

And whence had come *Aurora*? No one seemed to know except
Her wood was wet with Water from a River Time yclept.

And her name was not *Aurora*, but a stranger one had been—
The *Limb of Yggdrasill* upon her bowsprit they had seen.

Some said she set her sails to catch no ordinary breeze,
But winds that blew between the worlds, from off sidereal seas.

And now the ship was loading and the weight of her supplies
Had dropped her 'cross the water as the arctic skua flies.

Like marching armies, winged ships on ample galleys sail;
For lack of food her goal to reach, *Aurora* would not fail.

Into her yawning hold went bawling cattle live in droves,
And after them the produce of a hundred fields and groves.

Provisions for uncertain siege beyond the blue-walled rink
Where wood that yesterday had shaped would cross the crystal brink,

The edge of the world where restless seas forgot the warmth their childhood knew;
Where outstretched hands of stark, stripped trees had reached in vain for vanished blue.

The suits of fur and parka hoods, connoting colder clime,
The rawhide boots and leathern gloves were loaded at a time

When high a-sky the searing Sun with retroactive rays
Beat down on Ash that spongelike stored the heat for later days.

Then tools and paraphernalia with which men would cope with ice,
The clog-clad shoes and grappling hooks to break the rigid vise

The Torngat's icy hosts would use to crush *Aurora*'s hull,
With none to mourn her passing but the lonely skua gull.

The livelong day she loaded, far into the sultry night,
The endless work illumined by a summer moon and bright.

And when the whitened ramparts of the night had morning scaled,
Aurora weighed her anchor; out to sea she boldly sailed.

The little people gathered in the spendor of the morn
To wish the great ship godspeed and behold a world reborn.

He sails to fight the Northland's king, who clamped his icy yoke
Across the undefended Southlands, thus a gray one spoke.

And yet he has an ally in a Sun now full rearmed
To take the war to Kryochore, whose Ice King waits alarmed.

Who holds the Heartland holds the world, the Cold One oft has said;
The Fortress Ice Land's shores are strewn with well-intentioned dead,

The pitiful expendables who tried the Torngat's might
Now lie in twisted postures in the sempiternal night.

Can swift *Aurora*'s magic wood against the ice prevail?
Can Yggdrasill's enchanted Limb the frozen fort assail?

The light of morning blazened on the hope of mankind's sails,
And from the sea came echoing the laughter of the gales.

Against the sky her snowy sheets like mailed fists were hurled;
In all her rig no canvas scrap but to the wind unfurled.

And *Aurora,* which was morning, in the morning's light dissolved,
Assimilated by the Sun, though separately involved.

Atop the world, uneasy seated, the King of Kryochore
Had watched a Sun he thought defeated, reverse the tide of war
That overwhelmed the Shining One. He saw the weakened rays
Restored to twice their primal force in blinding, blistering blaze.
Where Carthage deep in time's dark womb was still infertile seed
The heavenly host of Flame and Fire the warmest Southland freed.
He drove the Ice King well beyond the Midtellurian Seas,
By hand to hand, from land to land, and up the Chersonese.
Deflated by the speed with which his outposts dissipated,
The Torngat drew behind his wall and patiently awaited
Invasion of the Sun he knew could not afford to wait,
But crush him in his Fortress must, and terms of peace dictate.
Abruptly from offensive to defensive forced was he,
Convinced the Fortress Ice Land now impregnable could be.
With characteristic diligence he placed along his Fort
A grisly glacier guarding every access to a port.
The waters of his coastline long were strewn with bergs unnumbered,
That ships that sought to beach themselves by ice might be encumbered.
On snowy fields his icy winds were ready and alert
To strip white sails with whiter gales and landings thus avert.
Where Norman kings had yet to tread the later fruited plains,
The brave who tried had mostly died in rigor for their pains.
But still a valiant few escaped with priceless cartographs
To plan the fall of the Western Wall and avenge their cenotaphs.
With fine precautions taken, still the indisputable proof
The Ice King must have blundered; his Fortress had no roof.

The winds that bore *Aurora* chopped the channel where the last
Of trepidating mankind fled the Ice King in the past
To stand in proud defiance on the tight and tiny isle
That checked the chilling challenge for the all-important while
The Sun, with vision clouded by the spots across his face,
Could forge anew his warbeams and redintegrate the race.

The captain of *Aurora* watched her masts like sabres drawn
And steep aslant with canvas, by the wind with aery brawn
And steely thew, against the bloodless flesh of Ice Land held,
While shadows shelved ten thousand years within him grimly welled.
He saw the beach, the moving wall, the last of mankind, ragged, fleeing
In open boats beyond the reach of conquering ice he now was seeing.

So long intrenched, this cancerous white, the body, tired, accepts
Its raucous growth as evolution, changing old concepts,
It even greets as revolution, hails the unclean spread
That daily claims a larger part till last the body's dead.
Now comes the moment of an age, when Retribution's sword
Must strike the shield from Evil, who by long injustice cored,
Has set himself in rugged strength and yet may turn the edge,
As deeply rooted hardwoods oft defy the woodsman's wedge.
Let righteousness then not assume the unbecoming role
Of sainted savior well before achievement of its goal.
But mindful of its precious stake as keeper of the flame,
It brooks no symbiotic peace to end a scoreless game.

A ceil of overcast concealing, Sun had fashioned white
And waneless blades of crystal-piercing incandescent light.
Such might a single sector of the Earth had never seen,
And only now *Aurora* felt the surge behind the screen.
Renascent vigor yet to taste the salty wine of fray;
Tellurian skies incarnadine or everlasting gray.
His strength the Cold One had amassed behind his Western Wall,
To there await whatever fate his Fortress might befall.
Supremely confident that Sun his spearhead bright would break;
Serenely well content that none a beachhead tight could take.
And then he spied a full-rigged ship with scintillating sails,
A ship that shed with fine contempt the onslaught of his gales.
Surprise was followed quickly by a staring disbelief—
Aurora's hull had crossed unharmed the underwater reef,
Stalagmites sharp, like teeth of glass, from channel floor protruding,
The lower jaws he counted on the ships of men extruding.
How dared this fragile wooden shell assault the Ice King's lair?
And whence this wind, a breath from hell, she carried in her hair?
Its scorching fingers seared his shores with dim-remembered heat;
The glinting snows that gemmed his crown were tarnished into sleet.

Now heeled before the vesicant wind, with quivering mast and plank
She hurled herself at Ice Land's white and thinly armored flank.
The surfused sea began to boil,
The sintered ice expanding
With a hollow roar that shook the shore
Where cliffs of chalk were standing,
Their faces blanched, the stinging bite
Of wrathful Sun's uncurling lash
Awaiting, rigid in the light,
The hyperpurple nivicidal wash.
Now heist!
The Torngat takes the measure of the Time-intended flying craft;
The feathered arrow surely launched from an olden archer's twanging bow.
The scraping peals the wind has lofted reach his ear. The Sun has laughed.
And laughter whets the cutting edge that strikes the first decisive blow.
To stay the tide he cannot fend beneath the Sun's unyielding glare,
He seeks with ice the ship to rend, to break her bones and beach her bare.
But O the Wood of Yggdrasill by standing water is not daunted—
Aurora cleaves the bergs in two, the Ice King's vanquished weapon vaunted.
No more the leaking sky affords an aery ambush for his winds
That, icy-pinioned, wheel and sweep the sullen ceil aslant the sea.
For Sun his fiery mantle o'er the knifing prow has spread,
And traps the ice winds shrieking, as they, dying, burning, flee.
The cliffs of chalk are crumbling now, attacked by fulminating rivers.
The sea itself is on the march, in metered tread, iambic quivers.
Great tremors trace the stricken strand,
The Earth splits wide asunder;
The fall of ice is quickened and
The heavens filled with thunder.
The Sun has moved the sky, now clear, within his hands a burning glass,
Across the white constrictor sheet that crushed the life from leaves of grass.
He strikes the stolid glaciers with unsated all-consuming fire,
The centuried concretion of his slowly cumulative ire
Repressed for ashen ages by the sickly spots upon his face,
Now clear-complexioned savior of the Earth's predestined ruling race.

Aurora's wings are folded and her men have headlong pushed ashore
Across pre-Norman tundra in the wetly waning wake of war.
To the measure of their booted feet the crossing hands move 'round the clock;
The curtain falls across the stage, the final act of Ragnarok.

The gods of snow and ice are dead; their king has died or fearful fled.
Persistent as one's old desires, an ancient chill from Earth suspires.
The newborn green that verds the land is not untouched by Torngat's hand;
The upraised palm exchanged, perhaps, for the clenched fist on future maps.
Laid to last ten thousand years, the crystal kingdom brashly broken
Had nonetheless its furrowed scars on growing granite rudely carved,
Reminding all the unborn years with ineradicable token
Of dark return in shaded lands that still for sunlight thinly starved.

Fourth Movement

What glory in the battle won if yet the cause is lost?
What triumph bright beneath the sun for him
who pays its cost?

IV. Finale.

Adagio lamentoso (♩=54)

affrettando

largamente

largamente

largamente

largamente

205

affrettando

Adagio lamentoso (♩=54)

Adagio lamentoso

O treacherous God! She does not live!
My long-lost love forever sleeping?
No more to wake, her brightness give
In sweet reunion, Time-tryst keeping?
O tell me not this fair white form,
Immobile, cold as arctic stone,
In vain has lain within this grot
Ten thousand empty years alone.
Has He who fills the maw of night
With souls from Earth protesting torn
By catlike stealth or unmasked might
This promised bride of birthright shorn?
Not mine the tryst, but His to keep.
The faceless Azrael's fleshless hand
In flouting God dishonors sleep
And contravenes divine command.
Poor mortal fools may sing His praise:
Komm süsser Todt—forgive their folly.
He is the worm in victory's fruit,
In triumph's cup the bitter lees.
When God's left hand, so clearly seen,
Has thus usurped His major role,
Dare I denounce the single part
And leave unscathed the blameful whole?

O ravished Star by lecherous Night!
Extinguished Sun in a jealous sky!
So silent now in waning white,
Ordained to live—condemned to die.

Andante

In the absence of angels the gods fashioned you
In their image and likeness—what else could they do?
Can heaven's handmaid compass then the total sum of such perfection
Yet leave for me no waiting warm in this your last and white reflection?
Where once I held a captured thing, a cloudlet soft in summer sky,
The wind has won with warring wing. Can they who made you let you die?
The lark has sung its final song; the last sweet note to earth descended;
To ruined skies you now belong; your hundred-centuried sleep has ended.

Long before our lips had met
Or shaped the words of love we spoke,
My heart was liquid in the warmth
With which your wondrous eyes caressed me.
The vibrant sweetness of your voice
Dulcet as a lonely lute
That hangs the fabric of its song
Against the cheerless wilderness.
And once I watched the burnished bronze
Of setting Sun's reluctant rays,
And knew he stole the rusty gold
While passing trusted through your hair.

Can you, once living, so long be dead
The years implant a reasoned doubt
The deathless light you onetime shed
Can linger when the lamp is out?

Beacon bright, forever dark!
Across the waveless watery waste,
The lightless limbo of the Stream,
Now let this heart be your companion.

Andante non tanto

O God to Whom unuttered prayers of searching mankind are addressed,
Confirm not what unwilling eyes have vainly hastened to reject.
This woman Thou created not to live a single span
But forever was Thy promise, if to Thee a promise kept.
Have I not her name remembered when remembrance was a crime
And loved her through the frozen years while ice-entombed she slept?
Can a cloud of dark dishonor shade the white face of All-High,
And heaven's house be sullied by the impact of a lie?
Wouldst Thou in Thy omnipotence the Stream of Time pervert,
By changing runes the Nornir writ, Thy Ragnarok avert?
Thou canst not take this gentle flower, so still ten thousand years
In deathless sleep. If Thou canst cry, O God where are Thy tears?
Are we to Thee then nothing more than actors in a play,
With borrowed burnings in our breasts and borrowed things to say?
Remember Thou, this murky world Thou deemst Thy proper stage
Was lit before the light of day had seen Thy countenance.
For in the gray unguarded hour with Reason's throne unsat,
The Son of Man preempted it with godly impudence.
Aye! Since the day Thy hand has moved Thy will to implement,
Not balanced by the logic checks that stay the rashest hand.
All unopposed Thy strength has grown by daily increment
Till none may now impugn the score, a true account demand.
O spendthrift Thou of fleeting Time! The silver centuries ring
Like coins within Thy fattened purse entreating to be spent.
Considering not the even worth expenditure should bring,
O canst Thou not remember that the coin was only lent?

Andante

Awake my love, I pray you. Let me look into the blue
Unmatched in all the firmament. Have I forgotten you?
How well do I remember, O so long a time ago,
I left you in this crystal cave and heard the West Wind moan
As soft your name it murmured, then in trauma left the shore
To wander o'er the darkened face of Earth forevermore—

On the edge of the world where restless seas
Whispered of warmth their childhood knew;
Where outstretched hands of stark stripped trees
Reached in vain for vanished blue.
And like the wind that seaward fled
I too was set adrift
But carried in a secret place the memory of your face.
I saw your portrait like a star
In every sunless sky
That roofed the countless times I crawled,
Unwalking, yet to die.
O who has counted footsteps vain, unnumbered milestones passed?
And who has charted reckless wakes that scar the ocean vast?
What glory in the battle won if yet the cause is lost?
What triumph bright beneath the sun for him who pays its cost?

To bloom no more, my sweetest flower
In all the gardens of the world?
The only seal upon your lids
The weight of morning dew empearled.
For when the Snow was conquered by
The advent of avenging Sun,
By century-sorcered alchemy
The Torngat's work was slow undone.
There is no trace upon your face;
The Ice has left no lasting mark.
The Southland's rose is in your cheek,
The song of birds now bids you hark.
What then restrains, constrains and binds
You in this breathless deathlike state?
What hand erased the runes of stone
On which was writ your storied fate?
I know.
You are dead.
You have for all time died.
Your fragile craft all access to the River-Sea denied.
The greening Earth,
The blue-filled skies,
The yellow warmth of summer sun
Cannot contrive to greet your eyes—
The years have left you, one by one.

O have you died with memory?
Or walk you eyeless in a void—
A candleflame in tenebrae,
A small and lonely asteroid.
What thrice-familiar forms that moved across your once retentive screen
Have joined the unremembered dead, impressed thereon no major scene?
Anamnesis is of consciousness a sustaining facet, not a phase,
And consciousness the measure of the River's depth and pulsing flow,
That fixes not on planes of years but on the nextness of its days,
Perceiving not this simple fact: the watershed must also grow.

The wetly hovering walls return the aching shadow of my words.
And as I speak I know I am my one and only listener.
A scream to God, a whispered threat, a tentatively burgeoned prayer,
Like homing birds released afar, come back to roost within my ear.
The winds that blow between the worlds have tasted silence vast and deep
In soundless voids where fetal spheres are rocked in embryonic sleep.
O blow ye winds upon these ears and let no more the fretful wave
Incite their ready tympana till I have sought my final grave.
O sacrilegious sight that seeks the splendor of the rising sun,
When eyes imprisoned darkly 'neath the ponderous depth of glacial blue,
Though rescued from the incubus of hundred-centuried leaden sleep,
Have slipped into a deeper dream from which the dreamer never wakes.
The bony sockets of my skull, let these be dry and empty cups
Of seeing purged by shorter waves that ride the combers of the day,
That I may walk in endless night, eternal unrelenting black
As that oblique oblivion where the best of Earth is put away.
I well might use my phalanged strength to speed me from the temporal Sea,
And scuttling thus my battered craft, find arid peace in vacuo.
Recalling yet on many a lane the times the turnstile turned for me,
Who can wonder that I know for me death has no permanence.
If not by mine, then by whose hand shall I be sent from worlds I know
To angled ones not tangent to the planes of cosmic consciousness?
To Him Who sits the manmade throne I've made my last and vain appeal—
His eyes are glass. His ears are stone. His heart of metal cannot feel.
Then from the hinter fields that flank the neatly disked and seeded memory,
I hear a voice both sad and sweet, as if its speech had caused it pain
And touched with timeless echoes of a million contemplative years,
"Turned never once in all the flow, to seek the Dweller on the plain."

Yggdrasill! O Mother-Tree!
How well I've earned Thy sad reproach,
Who generously has shown Her son the stones that shaped the River's course,
And gladly lent what I have spent in vain return to yesteryear
That I might find salvation in a still uncharted Waterway.
The arching sky, our heaven's concept, stretching high above our heads
Is tightly held to spinning Earth by Thy prehensile, faithful limbs,
Or else the wispy envelope, the envy of the hungry winds
That roam the airless voids, would yield brief revel with our breath.
The wounded bird that like a plummet falls from out his ocean thin
And feels the downward shoreward pull of Thy relentless finger's beck
Cannot condemn the raking grasp that till the moment of his fall
Had filled his lungs with aery pulse and placed a carpet under him.
Could we but stand in outer space, from some impossible vantage see
Telluria's rugged countenance, her soaring peaks and desert plains,
Beneath the rumpled skin on which our temporary tents we pitch
Behold the primal force that molds our finite world with infinite pains.

Thy roots engird the planet's waist,
With strengthening hands its backbone braced.
Thou art the law, yet none less prone
Than Thee to break the law Thou art.
Couldst Thou Thy littlest finger crook,
A local tremor leave untraced,
And yet the sacrosanct of law
Remain unbroke in every part?
Close then the door of this sorrowing cave.
Let me die with my love. Let here be my grave.
Shake and abandon this wet rocky tomb.
Seal it and leave it in Night's fruitless womb,
That ever and ever, forever on end,
In lightless oblivion I endlessly spend.

Hardly the words by my lips have been uttered
When Earth has fantastically shivered and shuddered.
Saxifragous forces tightly have sealed
The single low entrance, around me congealed
The air like a solid, and breathing comes hard
As aeriform atoms are jolted and jarred.

In the moments that follow the air soon is spent,
And the life it supported no longer is pent
In a temple reluctant, but escapes like a sigh,
As a ship slips its moorings; thus gladly I die.
I hold fast my loved one in long last embrace,
And even in darkness I still see her face.
Then a rustle, a stirring—she raises her head—
O God! It is too late—
For I now am dead.

Designed by Victor A. Curran

Text composed in 12-point Benedictine Book by the Monotype Composition Company, Baltimore, Maryland

Display composed in Mergenthaler Cochin by Dean's Composition, Baltimore, Maryland

Printed on 80-pound Bay Opaque Smooth by Universal Lithographers, Inc., Timonium, Maryland

Bound in Joanna Buckram by the Delmar Printing Company, Charlotte, North Carolina

Bound in paper by Perfect Books, Inc., Baltimore, Maryland